MW01094700

Hey Kids! Let's Visit Charleston South Carolina

Teresa Mills

Life Experiences Publishing

Bluff City, Tennessee

Teresa Mills/Life Experiences Publishing
PO Box 53
Bluff City, TN 37618
www.kid-friendly-family-vacations.com

Book Layout © 2014 BookDesignTemplates.com

Hey Kids! Let's Visit Charleston South Carolina/Teresa Mills -- 1st ed.
ISBN - 978-1-946049-04-9

Contents

Preface

Welcome

Charleston, South Carolina, is one of the most beautiful Southern cities in the United States! Charleston is on a peninsula, so there are rivers on both sides and great views. Like so many other places that you can visit, there are just so many things to do and see there.

This book is written as a fun fact guide about several Charleston attractions and sites. Throughout the book you'll find some history interspersed with fun facts about things to do in the city. Parents can either read the book with their children or have their children read it themselves.

You can visit Charleston, South Carolina, right from your own home with this book! You can enjoy this book whether you are preparing for a vacation with the family and want to learn more about the city or just wanting to learn a little more about Charleston.

When you take your family trip to Charleston, I have a free gift to help you plan! Go to this link to receive your gift:

http://kid-friendly-family-vacations.com/charlestonattractions

When you have completed this book, I invite you to visit the other books in the series:

Hey Kids! Let's Visit Washington, DC
Hey Kids! Let's Visit a Cruise Ship
Hey Kids! Let's Visit New York City
Hey Kids! Let's Visit London, England
Hey Kids! Let's Visit San Francisco
Hey Kids! Let's Visit Savannah, Georgia
Hey Kids! Let's Visit Paris, France

Enjoy!

Teresa Mills

Introduction

A Little About Charleston South Carolina

South Carolina is one of the thirteen original colonies. Charleston is the biggest and oldest city in South Carolina, having gotten its name from King Charles II of England (1660 – 1685).

Charleston is known for being the Holy City because of its churches. These churches add to the city's charm, and the fact that it's considered "holy" makes ghost tours more interesting (if that's your thing).

Charleston is the place where the first shot was fired signaling the start of the US Civil War. It is also home to the longest cable-stayed bridge in North America, which spans the Charleston Harbor.

Charleston's downtown area is a great place to tour. There are horse-drawn carriage tours and many other types of tours, some of which I cover in the book. You can also rent bicycles and ride through the downtown area on your own.

There is just so much to learn about and see in Charleston. There is so much history in Charleston to soak up that learning as much as you can before visiting will really make the trip more fun.

So, are you ready?

Let's visit Charleston, South Carolina!

1

Charleston Visitor Center

The Charleston Visitor Center, or Charleston Visitor Reception and Transportation Center, is the first place to go when visiting Charleston. Located at 375 Meeting Street, this historical landmark was built in the mid 1800s. After a series of renovations to restore the landmark, the building finally opened its doors to the public on May 1991 as the Charleston Visitor Center.

The Charleston Visitor Center is the place to go to find out about the variety of tours and activities that are available throughout Charleston. Their friendly staff members are well informed and trained in assisting visitors. They can also help you in planning tours and activities based on what you and your family want to see and do.

They are open seven days a week from 8:30 a.m. to 5:30 p.m. except for Christmas, New Year, and Thanksgiving Day.

The center has a theater that shows a short film about the history and culture of Charleston. A thirty-six-minute film titled *Forever Charleston* airs also every forty-five minutes. The film features places around Charleston and some significant historical facts about the city.

The Visitor Center staff can help you with recommendations on things to see, places to eat, and even hotels in the areas.

Facts about the Charleston Visitor Center

- Construction on the building was done in stages beginning in 1840 and completed in 1856.

- It is among five railroad buildings that are collectively known as William Aiken House & Associated Railroad Structures, and named a National Historic Landmark District.

- It opened to the public in 1991, following an extensive renovation that used a lot of materials from the original structure.

2

Fort Sumter National Monument

Fort Sumter off the coast of Charleston is where the US Civil War started. The Confederates took the fort in only thirty-four hours, and the Union tried for four years to get it back.

Construction on Fort Sumter started in 1829, and was still incomplete in 1861 when the Civil War began. The fort has five sides and was built to accommodate 650 men and 135 guns. The fort was built after the war of 1812 as a series of forts to protect the US coastline.

Fort Sumter

The tour at the fort is self-guided, but there are national park rangers available for questions. The tour includes a lot of history about the significance of the fort in the Civil War. This is a great way to soak up the Civil War history that is such a big part of the South.

There are Civil War–era cannons on display at the fort. In addition, you can tour old barracks and get a feel for the distance to the Charleston Harbor from the fort.

Fort Sumter Cannons

Tours are handled by Spirit Line Cruises, and de-
part from Liberty Square at the Aquarium Wharf,
or from Patriot's Point in Mt. Pleasant. Spirit Lines
offers the only commercial boat transportation to
Fort Sumter, the island fort where the Civil War
began. The 2 hour 15 minute tour consists of ap-
proximately 1 hour at Fort Sumter, then a 1 hour
and 15 minute cruise around Charleston's historic
harbor. The tours run daily except for Thanksgiving Day, Christmas Day, and New Years Day.

Fun Facts about Fort Sumter

- Did you know that this was where the Civil War in America started? When conflict arose between the Northern and American factions in 1861, the first shots from the Confederates were fired from this fort.

- The fort is named after General Thomas Sumter, a Revolutionary War hero.

- Seventy thousand tons of granite were imported from New England to build up a sandbar on which to build the fort.

3

Battery & White Point Gardens

One of Charleston's most historic spots is an area collectively known as the Battery & White Point Gardens. The Battery is a landmark promenade and defensive seawall that stretches along the Charleston peninsula's lower shores, bordered by the Cooper and Ashley rivers. The White Points Gardens is a 2.3-hectare (5.7-acre) public park located within the Battery.

The peaceful park and promenade offers great views of Fort Sumter and the Charleston Harbor. Look back across the street and you will see some elegant Charleston mansions. Gigantic oak trees provide shade at White Point Gardens where kids can play on the Civil War–era cannons and weapons displayed there.

Since 1837, the Battery & White Point Gardens have been used as a public garden. Special events like weddings are frequently held at the beautiful white gazebo at the park's center.

Walking along the Battery is a great way to spend part of an afternoon in Charleston. There are also many historic walking tours that include the Charleston Battery area.

The Charleston Battery

Fun Facts about the Battery & White Point Gardens

- The city of Charleston started to develop near the Battery, which is where passengers sailing into the harbor were welcomed. At the peninsula's tip, local Indians discarded lots of white oyster shells, which is where the name White Point came from.

- Under the Battery's shady oak trees is a stone monument that informs visitors that White Point used to be a location of many pirates' executions. Long ago, over a five-week period, about fifty pirates were hanged under the oak trees. One of those hanged was Stede Bonnet, the infamous "gentleman pirate" (he was a landowner before turning to a life of crime). He was buried in a marsh nearby.

- As the Civil War broke out, the Battery & White Point Gardens became a city fortification. Nowadays, there's an impressive display of historic cannons and mortars from the Civil War used to defend and shell the city. There's a Confederate mon-

ument at the corner of East Bay and Mur-
ray.

- Around 1770, stunning mansions were
  built, and the area's ugly history is
  eclipsed by its beauty today. Many of the
  mansions are still around, and they draw
  in a lot of tourists.

4

Riley Waterfront Park

As former Charleston mayor Joseph P. Riley Jr. says, the Waterfront Park in the city's downtown area is like an outdoor cathedral surrounded by stars and sky, water and trees, and the downtown Charleston skyline. The park is attributed to the former mayor.

Completed in May 1990, the park measures thirteen acres. It provides visitors and residents alike a public sanctuary where they can sit and relax, and enjoy views of the Cooper River. Here, kids can play in the interactive water-and-spray fountains. Visitors can also stroll along the waterfront promenade under mature oak trees.

Riley Waterfront Park

Waterfront Park was recognized in 2007 by the National Trust for Historic Preservation and the American Society of Landscape Architects with a Landmark Award, which distinguishes landscape architecture examples that contribute to the public landscape's beauty.

The park's location—between Adger's Wharf and Vendue Range—was historically a maritime traffic center with shipping terminals and several wharves. The area had been in decline for decades. In June 1955, a fire occurred at a steamship terminal in the area. By 1980, the area was marred by gravel parking lots and charred pilings.

The then-Mayor Riley started planning for a park as he first became mayor in 1975. Land acquisition started in 1979, and in 1988, the project broke ground. A September 1989 hurricane struck the city, causing damage to Waterfront Park. The park nevertheless opened in May 1990.

Fun Facts about Waterfront Park

- Built along classic lines and with durable materials, the park has bronze castings of historic maps that show different stages of the development of the city. There are also fountains made of cast stone, bronze, and granite. The park's center has a fountain featuring a golden pineapple while the pier has "Charleston chairs," with each chair big enough to hold a family.

- The park, which is located in downtown Charleston, provides visitors with a place of quiet that is contrasted with the nearby commercial and busier areas of the downtown area. My family and I have even spent time playing Duck, Duck, Goose in the park!

- Riley Waterfront Park has been a vital part of Charleston's $400 million downtown revitalization that got private capital of $337 million, or a return of $4.62 on each invested public dollar.

5

Charleston City Market

The historic Charleston City Market was constructed on land ceded in 1788 by Charles
Cotesworth Pinckney—a Revolutionary War vet-
eran—to the city of Charleston.

A condition on ceding the land was that it be uti-
lized always as a public market. Now, the market
is home to unique, small shops selling local goods
like artwork, sweetgrass baskets, woven baskets,
jewelry, vegetables, and fruits.

In 1807, the market was established, and until
the 1930s it was the place to find meat, vegeta-
ble, and fish vendors. In 1840, the current
structure, with its entrance that faces Meeting
Street, was built. Inside, you will find four blocks
of open-air space with various vendors.

Charleston City Market

The historic market is perhaps downtown Charleston's most visited shopping destination. It's open year-round, and is always bustling with sightseers and shoppers. In 2011, it underwent a major renovation. It now features revolving fans and air-conditioning.

The market is located at 188 Meeting Street and intersects with Market Street. The market's central location makes it accessible on foot from the cruise ship terminal and from most downtown guest houses and hotels.

Fun Facts about the Charleston City Market

- The market stretches for 380 meters (1,240 feet) through multiple sheds oriented east-to-west. Stalls occupy Market Hall's first story and continue through a shed that stretches from the hall's rear to Church Street. The sheds, since their nineteenth-century completion, have been rebuilt and renovated multiple times due to damage from fires, earthquakes, tornadoes, and other disasters.

- The market's main building, the Greek Revival–style Market Hall, has one raised story above a rustic, open ground-level arcade. Roman and Greek temples, like the Temple of Athena Nike and the Temple of Portunus, inspired the building's frontal portico and high base.

- The market is often referred to as "Slave Market." Why? Slaves of the past would buy food for their respective plantations. Now, the market is filled with visitors and residents alike, looking through stalls loaded with clothes, toys, regional souvenirs, and leather goods. The "basket ladies" are a must-see. For centuries, they have been weaving baskets using local materials like palmetto leaves and sweet-grass.

6

Confederate Museum

The Confederate Museum, located between Meeting and East Bay streets, is a Greek Revival landmark. Formerly called Market Hall, the museum is home to Charleston Chapter #4, the Daughters of the Confederacy. It offers Civil War history and tours.

The museum is open for visitors all year round, Tuesdays to Saturdays, from 11:00 a.m. to 3:30 p.m.

The museum is on the top floor of the City Market.

Confederate Museum – Above the City Market

The Confederate Museum used to be the central place for commercial activities in Charleston, hence its former name, Market Hall. The market commissioners used the upper part of the hall as their headquarters. Upstairs, there were two small rooms for business transactions, and another room, which was larger, was where meetings and social functions were conducted.

In 1894, the Daughters of the Confederacy was born. To this day, this hall serves as their headquarters. The ladies started collecting relics from the war, and as their collections grew, a permanent place for display was needed. The Confederate Museum was selected to be used for that purpose. The museum opened for visitors and tours in 1899.

Fun Facts about the Confederate Museum

- The building that houses the museum is a National Historical Landmark, and is one of the best examples of Greek Revival–style architecture.

- On display in the museum are Confederate uniforms, cannons, swords, and flags.

- This is the place where soldiers enlisted for the Confederate Army.

7

Old Slave Mart Museum

The Old Slave Mart Museum, formerly a building in the complex of buildings called Ryan's Mart, may be the only surviving building once used for slave auctions in the South. Slave auction activities in this building ended in 1863. The museum is located at 6 Chalmers Street.

This slave-trade building was constructed in 1859. To its west, the building was supported by the German Fire Hall walls. Inside was a large room that had a ceiling twenty feet high. The front of the building featured an iron gate, octagonal pillars, and an arch.

Prior to 1856, slaves were held and sold at the Custom House, now the Exchange Building. Public sales were prohibited that year, resulting in private trades of slaves in rooms, yards, and marts. One of those marts belonged to Thomas Ryan.

The property was then sold in 1859 to a Mr. Oakes, who continued the trade until the Civil War that led to the abolishment of slavery.

Around 1878, the building underwent a renovation that turned it into a two-story house, and in 1938, Miriam Wilson bought the property. He transformed the building into a site for African American arts, crafts, and history.

Fun Facts about the Old Slave Mart Museum

- The name Gullah came from the word Angola, the African region where 40 percent of slaves sold in the Charleston Market originated.

- In February 1865, when Charleston was occupied by the Union forces, slaves were found imprisoned right in this museum's building, then called Ryan's Mart.

- There is a parking lot in the current site right behind the building. This used to contain a kitchen and the barracoon, meaning "slave jail" in the Spanish language.

8

Old Exchange & Provost Dungeon

Charleston is the largest and oldest city in South Carolina. Because of its long history, a lot of historical "gems" are tucked away in this beautiful city, one of which is the Old Exchange & Provost Dungeon. It is located at 122 East Bay Street. Its construction lasted from 1767 to 1771.

Unlike the other historical landmarks, which were the private residences of Charleston's prominent families, this building started out as a public building and still remains as one today. It is now a museum and is currently owned by the South Carolina Society of the Daughters of the American Revolution.

Old Exchange and Provost Dungeon

The Old Exchange & Provost Dungeon Building is open from 9:00 a.m. to 5:00 p.m. every day. Visitors are welcome to drop by to enjoy and re-live the colorful history of South Carolina. The museum also has educational programs open to kids and adults.

Fun Facts about the Old Exchange & Provost Dungeon

- It is where the delegates of South Carolina to the First Continental Congress were elected in 1774.

- The First Continental Congress was a meeting of the delegates of the thirteen colonies. They met in Philadelphia, Penn-sylvania, from September 5, 1774, to October 26, 1774. The meeting was in re-sponse to a harsh law that the British Parliament passed during that time. The thirteen colonies present in the meeting were as follows: New Hampshire, Massa-chusetts, Rhode Island, Connecticut, New York, New Jersey, Pennsylvania, Delaware, Maryland, Virginia, North Carolina, and South Carolina.

- The delegates of South Carolina were Henry Middleton, Edward Rutledge, John Rutledge, Thomas Lynch Jr., and Christopher Gadsden. These delegates were elected in the Old Exchange & Provost Dungeon.

- The British used the cellar of the building as a prison during the Revolution.

- According to reports, there were too many prisoners of war during the Revolution that the British had no choice but to use the building as a prison cell. Around 120 South Carolina residents were thought to have been locked up in the Provost Dungeon under charges of sedition or treason.

- Pirates were also imprisoned here. Prior to the British using the Exchange Building as a prison, pirates were imprisoned here in 1718. It was a time when pirates ruled the ocean. They ransacked ship after ship, which took a great toll on the English shipping industry. As a result, the British government started a manhunt to track down the pirates. After catching them, they were imprisoned in the Exchange Building while awaiting execution.

- The Declaration of Independence was presented to the citizens and residents of South Carolina in the steps of this building.

9

Edmondston-Alston House

The Edmondston-Alston House is one of the Historical House Museums in Charleston. It has a beautiful view of the Charleston Harbor. This is the house where General Lee sought refuge on a night in December 1861 when a fire in a Charleston hotel where he was staying broke out.

The house was built in 1825 by Charles Edmondston, who at the time had a flourishing shipping business. For economic reasons, in 1837 Edmondston decided to sell it to a man named Charles Alston, a member of a rice-planting dynasty.

In the next two decades, the first floor of the house was used for business, and the Alston family lived in the upper floors. From the house, the

Alstons witnessed the unfolding of the events of the Civil War.

Fun Facts about the Edmondston-Alston House

- On the house's piazza, you can try a joggling boarding (a bench that is 10 to 16 feet long. The bench is a thin, pliable board that is supported on each end by wooden stands. The bench is long enough that it bounces, or jostles when you sit on it).

- During the first battle of the Civil War, the residents of the house held a party for family and friends. The party was purposely designed for these guests to see the attack on Fort Sumter.

- Charleston is full of tales of ghost appearances. The Edmondston-Alston House has its share of hair-raising ghost stories too.

10

The Calhoun Mansion

The Calhoun Mansion is a Charleston Landmark, constructed in 1876. The architect of this mansion was William P. Russell. It is dubbed as the "handsomest and most complete private residence in the South." This should be no surprise as the construction of the mansion cost $200,000. In addition, the land where the mansion sits was purchased for $40,000 Confederate dollars.

The Calhoun Mansion is open for tours every day from 11:00 a.m. to 5:00 p.m., except on Thanksgiving Day and Christmas Day. The regular tour usually lasts from half an hour to an hour, while the grand tour usually lasts for an hour and a half.

Fun Facts about the Calhoun Mansion

- It is ginormous. It is a large estate. It is over 24,000 square feet and has thirty-five rooms. It has a grand ballroom, private elevators, Japanese water gardens, koi ponds, and piazzas.

- This museum is still the primary residence of its current owner, who lives on the third floor of the mansion. The first and second floors are the ones open for touring. During a tour of the mansion, visitors will get a glimpse of the massive collection of antiques belonging to current and previous owners.

- After the original owner, George W. Williams, died, the ownership of the house was passed from person to person. Because of this, the condition of the house deteriorated, leading to it being condemned by the city government. However, through the initiative of a Charleston local, the mansion was restored. The restoration cost $5 million.

- It was used as the set for Nicholas Spark's movie *The Notebook*. The interior shots of the house of the female lead character Rachel's parents were filmed inside the mansion.

11

Dock Street Theater

Dock Street Theater is located at 135 Church Street in Charleston's French Quarter neighborhood. It is the first building in the United States that was designed to be used exclusively as a theater.

The theater's curtains have "opened" three times. The first time was on February 2, 1736. The theater opened with a performance of *The Recruiting Officer*. A great fire in 1740 consumed the theater, along with other buildings in the area.

Planter's Hotel then rose in its place in 1803. The hotel did not stray far from its roots. It housed several famous actors and actresses as well as stage troupes during its time. The Civil War destroyed the hotel. The theater again opened its doors on November 26, 1937. The theater was modeled after eighteenth-century playhouses by architect Albert Simons. The theater stood in the hotel's courtyard. Curtains went down anew on the theater in 2007. For the next three years, the theater remained closed to undergo a massive renovation project.

Dock Street Theater and the French Quarter

[The theater is to the left in this photo of the French Quarter.]

The third opening took place on March 18, 2010. The renovations for the place amounted to a hefty $19 million. This was shouldered by the city government of Charleston.

At present, the theater caters to fifty thousand patrons. It produces over one hundred performances per season, aside from the school performances by South Carolina students.

Despite modernization, the theater has kept its old charm. Tourists will definitely enjoy the beautiful architecture of the theater. On certain days, tourists can also have backstage access. They will have the opportunity to see the life on the other side of the curtain. For paranormal enthusiasts, there are also ghost tours featuring the Dock Street Theater and other landmarks of Charleston.

Fun Facts about the Dock Street Theater

- The theater has been listed in the National Register of Historic Places since 1973. The National Register of Historic Places is a federal government list that contains structures deemed worthy of preservation.

- The first opera performance in America, *Flora*, took place in this theater. Flora was featured in Dock Street Theater on February 8, 1735. Flora was a popular ballad from England at that time. It captured the imagination of the colonies.

- Junius Brutus Booth, famous nineteenth-century actor, worked and stayed in Planter's Hotel. Another notable individual who worked in Planter's Hotel was Robert Smalls, an African American war hero. He was a waiter at Planter's Hotel before the war.

12

Rainbow Row

One of the most photographed landmarks in Charleston is the Rainbow Row.

Rainbow Row is a row of Georgian houses painted in the colors of the rainbow. There are thirteen houses in total, and the row is located on Tradd Street, Elliot Street, and East Bay Street. The houses faced the Cooper River in 1740. However, that location was subsequently destroyed during the Civil War.

In the 1920s, Susan Pringle Frost purchased six buildings to restore them. But she did not have enough money to restore all six houses. Susan Pringle Frost is the founder of the Society for the Preservation of Old Dwellings.

In 1931, Dorothy Haskell Porcher Legge bought a section of the houses and renovated them. Most of the houses were restored to their original condition by 1945.

Rainbow Row

Fun Facts about Rainbow Row

- There are many myths as to why the houses are painted in the colors of the rainbow. One myth says that the houses were colored so that drunken sailors would know which house they lived in. Others say that it was a way for the merchants to advertise their businesses. Another theory says that the houses were painted in pastel to keep the temperature in the houses cool.

- It is one of the most "Instagrammed" sites in Charleston. Currently, the hashtag "rainbowrow" and the place "Rainbow Row" are the most popular.

- Not all the houses were built and restored at the same time. As mentioned, the row houses were destroyed during the Civil War. House number 79 is the southern-most and newest home. It was built in 1845. The house number 85 on East Bay Street was the last to be restored. House number 97 on East Bay Street. was the first to be restored by Legge. Number 105 is the only house with a Victorian front, and house number 107 has a two-story kitchen house. Number 89 is the only row house that has a side garden.

13

Children's Museum of the Lowcountry

Children's Museum of the Lowcountry, or CML, is an interactive learning museum for kids age ten and younger. CML is a nonprofit organization that allows children to play while learning. Located at 25 Ann Street, Children's Museum of the Lowcountry offers tons of activities that the whole family can enjoy.

One of the most unique and interesting features of the CML is the Art Room, which offers four different areas with tons of fun activities. First is the Creation Station where children can try problem solving and spatial awareness through creating art by using recyclable materials. The Painting Place is also a cool feature in the Art Room where your children can paint and learn how to interpret their work. The Discovery Den, on the other hand, focuses on new art forms, such as collage, weaving, and sculpting, that encourage your child to try new things to stimulate their imaginations. The Art Room also caters to very young children in the Sensory Space, an area where their speech and color recognition is enhanced through various activities.

Through the collaboration of CML and the Charleston Jazz Orchestra, the Swing! Exhibit was created. Swing! is a music-inspired section of the museum filled with different activities where the whole family can learn about the history and culture of jazz music.

There are literally thousands of possibilities and hundreds of activities at the Children's Museum of the Lowcountry. Additional features and exhibits include the Kids' Garden, the Fire Truck, Waterwise, and the Publix Market.

Fun Facts about the Children's Museum of the Lowcountry

- The Medieval Creativity Castle at the CLM is a great place to use your imagination. The castle has a puppet theater where your children can act out famous fairy ta-

les or even create their own unique fairy
tales.

- One fun, cool activity at the museum are
the horses at the Medieval Creative Castle.
You can feed and pet the horses.

- Kids can also dress like real firefighters on
the Fire Truck while learning about fire
safety.

14

South Carolina Aquarium

The South Carolina Aquarium is a great place to explore South Carolina's native plants and animals. It is a 93,000-square-foot infrastructure with different exhibits. You will find a bunch of exhibits from forestry to swamp grounds, as well as a huge aquarium with hundreds of animals and aquatic creatures.

The South Carolina Aquarium features a three-story aquarium. This aquarium contains more than seven hundred sea creatures.

There is also the Mountain Forest exhibit with flying bald eagles—a cool way to learn about the great bald eagle. The Mountain Forest exhibit also has a waterfall and a flowing river where you can see river otters swimming and snoozing around.

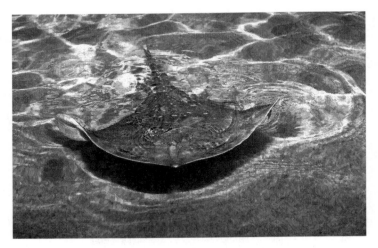

Stingray

The Coastal Plain is another cool exhibit. Here you will experience firsthand what it is like to be in a swamp. See how alligators wrestle and what their environment is like. You can also view different animals like the dreaded rattlesnake. It also features a number of plant species like the carnivorous Venus flytrap.

The Saltmarsh Aviary exhibit features interesting activities like feeding stingrays. It has a six-thousand-gallon stingray tank where you can feed the stingrays with shrimp. The Saltmarsh

Aviary exhibit also houses various other creatures like herons, the poisonous puffer fish, and the diamondback terrapin.

Fun Facts about the South Carolina Aquarium

- The touch tank is where you can touch and interact with different aquatic animals like hermit crabs, horseshoe crabs, sea urchins, whelks, and Atlantic stingrays.

- The second floor features Bricks Alive. There you'll find animals made from colorful LEGO bricks, including an eight-foot dolphin, a sea turtle, a bald eagle, and many more. This exhibit took more than five months to build, and the collection is still growing.

- The aquarium holds over 385,000 gallons of water.

15

Patriots Point Naval & Maritime Museum

Patriots Point Naval & Maritime Museum is a collection of four ships and twenty-five aircraft carriers. The 888-foot aircraft carrier Yorktown is the flagship of the battle group. Destroyer Laffey, the Coast Guard cutter Ingham, and the submarine Clamagore are also on display along with the aircraft that are displayed on the Yorktown.

The USS Clamagore is an iconic Cold War–era submarine. No other Guppy III submarine has been preserved in the US.

Known as "the ship that wouldn't die," the USS Laffey is another popular feature at the museum. It is the most decorated among all World War II–era US destroyers that are still in existence.

The USS Clamagore

The USS Yorktown—an actual naval aircraft carrier that can be explored by museum visitors—there are several walking tours throughout the vessel so that you can see all of the living and working quarters.

Another fun option available is camping on the USS Yorktown—yep, you spend the night onboard the ship!

The museum will manage your stay and take care of all food during the campout. All you have to do is make your reservations!

The museum also offers simulated flight lessons for kids.

The USS Yorktown

Fun Facts about Patriots Point

- Launched in 1943, the USS Yorktown is a naval vessel used by the American military during the Second World War. It was one of the largest ships used by the navy, complete with some of the most advanced equipment available at the time. It was one of twenty-four aircraft carriers built for World War II.

- There is a flight academy at the Patriots Point Naval & Maritime Museum where kids can participate in flight simulations handled by real-life military pilots.

- The museum is also an embarkation point for the boat ride to Fort Sumter.

16

Arthur Ravenel Jr. Bridge

The Arthur Ravenel Jr. Bridge connects Charleston and Mount Pleasant. It crosses the Cooper River.

The first bridge constructed to cross the Cooper River was the 4.3-kilometer Grace Memorial Bridge. It was a privately-owned bridge that charged a one-dollar toll for cars to cross. Tolls were stopped in 1946 after the bridge was purchased by South Carolina in 1943.

When tolls were stopped, the bridge started to deteriorate. Citing insufficient capacity and reduced lane width, the government constructed another bridge in 1966, the Pearman Bridge, to run alongside the older Grace Bridge. By 1979, because of lack of maintenance, the two bridges were declared functionally obsolete.

Ravenel Bridge

Construction of a new bridge was proposed, later to be named Arthur Ravenel Jr. Bridge. The bridge was named after the congressman who pushed for funding support from different agencies. Overall cost to finish the project was $700 million. The Federal Highway Administration and the State Infrastructure Bank shouldered the majority of the funding.

Fun Facts about the Arthur Ravenel Jr Bridge

- Not one company handled the construction of the bridge. There were actually several companies that split the project into five smaller projects.

- To build the foundations of the bridge, it took the crews one year. It took a few more years to build the towers and the deck.

- The Cooper River Bridge Run is held every year in April.

- The bridge has a really nice walking/biking path on one side. It is always busy.

17

Magnolia Plantation and Gardens

The 464-acre Magnolia Plantation and Gardens is located at 3550 Ashley River Road in Charleston County. It is among the oldest plantations in the South. The estate is on the National Register of Historic Places.

Thomas Drayton came from Barbados with his wife, Ann, in 1676. They landed at the new Charles Towne English colony. It is where they established the Magnolia Plantation. Thomas and Ann were the first in a long line of the plantation's direct family ownership. After more than three hundred years, the estate is still owned by direct descendants.

Magnolia Plantation and Gardens

During the Colonial era, the Magnolia Plantation experienced tremendous growth and wealth by cultivating rice. British and American troops would later occupy the property during the American Revolution. The Drayton sons then became statesmen and soldiers. They helped drive the British forces away.

In the latter part of the seventeenth century, the Draytons added gardens to the property. Grand-scale expansion and beautification efforts continued through the eighteenth century. In 1870, the Magnolia Plantation and Gardens first opened its doors to the public to help in the preservation and restoration of the historic estate.

The Drayton house has been preserved, and visitors can take a tour of the official Drayton home if they wish. Rooms have retained their original features, including the furniture, fixtures, and even the old linens. Through the garden tours, children can also learn about different plants and how to take care of them.

A variety of youth programs are also available. There are merit badge programs for Scouts, and parents can arrange for a camping adventure for the entire family. Admission fees are very affordable. The best part is that all kids age six and under can enjoy all the facilities free of charge.

Fun Facts about the Magnolia Plantation & Gardens

- A popular publication featured the Magnolia Plantation & Gardens as one of the most beautiful gardens in the entire country. No other garden in South Carolina has ever received such an honor.

- The plantation has always belonged to the Drayton family, who lived there for several generations—even after the property's conversion into a public park. It first came to life during the 1600s. It has since been transformed into a leisure spot for the public to enjoy, opening its doors in 1870.

- The Magnolia Plantation & Gardens was around a long time before the American Revolution, not to mention the Civil War.

18

Middleton Place

Middleton Place in Charleston used to be a rice plantation. It contains several attractions: the Gardens, Plantation Stableyards, and the Museum.

The Gardens are considered America's oldest landscaped gardens. Visitors can explore the sculptures, walkways, canals, architectural elements, and horticulture. Visitors can also tour the House Museum, where they can learn about the people who constructed and lived in Middleton Place.

The gardens mirror the symmetry of seventeenth-century European design. Parterres (an ornamental garden with paths between the beds), sculpted terraces, and reflection pools with swans highlight the garden's complicated design. In the winter, rare camellias grow. In the spring, azaleas cover the hillside overlooking Rice Mill Pond.

Middleton Place

John Williams, in the 1730s, started to build his house. He died after construction was completed. In 1741, his daughter Mary married Henry Middleton, who made changes to the land and house. Henry and Simms (no first name – only Simms), an English gardener, designed the luxurious garden.

Arthur Middleton, the son of Henry and Mary and a Declaration of Independence signer, became the owner in 1761. However, in 1780, British troops looted Middleton Place and destroyed its architectural elements. Arthur's oldest son, Henry inherited Middleton Place in 1787.

Henry's oldest son, Williams, became the owner in 1846 when his father died. An earthquake destroyed the Middleton Place three years after Williams died in 1883. In 1900, Elizabeth, Williams' daughter, began to restore the place. When she died in 1915, the place went to John Julius Pringle Smith. He and his wife, Heningham, restored the entire plantation and the gardens' layout. The Smiths had opened the gardens to the public by the 1920s. They later restored the house's historic charm.

The National Register of Historic Places recognized Middleton Place in 1971. The Middleton Place Foundation now owns the old plantation.

Fun Facts about Middleton Place

- In the stableyards, the slaves took care of the animals and did basic chores. A tour of the stableyards gives a glance into slavery during the eighteenth and nineteenth centuries.

- The British troops, in 1873, signed an agreement for surrender at Middleton Place.

- Arthur imported the first water buffalo, which he brought to Middleton Place. The animals were imported from Constantinople. Arthur and a friend, Andre Michaux, planted the country's first camellias.

- Middleton Place was where Williams Middleton signed the Ordinance of Secession. This action led to the Fort Sumter attack and the Civil War. Union forces burned Middleton Place. They also ate half the water buffalo population and transported the rest to what is now known as the Central Park Zoo in New York City.

19

Charles Towne Landing State Historic Site

Charles Towne Landing State Historic Site is located on a marshy point off the Ashley River. It sits on the original site where the first English settlers established the Carolina colony in 1670. Charles Towne Landing first opened in 1970, in celebration of the state of South Carolina's tricentennial.

The 664-acre historic site gives visitors a glimpse into Charleston's earliest colonial history. It houses an exhibit hall, a natural habitat zoo, miles of trails, a tall replica ship, dozens of picnic tables, six working cannons, ongoing archaeological excavations, and a lot more.

At the Visitor Center, families can take a look at the different exhibits available on-site. These exhibits are immersive (make you feel like you are actually part of the exhibit), making them ideal for young children and interesting enough for the rest of the family.

A history trail audio tour is also available at the Charles Towne Landing State Historic Site. The audio tour will provide you with plenty of information. It is self-guided, but there are maps and marked trails available. This is one of the immersive experiences at Charles Towne landing.

One of the more popular exhibits at the historic site is the Adventure, a replica of a seventeeth-century ship. You can also find war-era cannons inside the park. These are the actual cannons used by American soldiers. They are fired every now and then.

Preservation of the cannons is ongoing. There is also an animal forest within the park. This habitat zoo houses all sorts of animals, including bears and bison, to name a few.

Fun Facts about Charles Towne Landing

- One of the best views that you'll get once you visit the Charles Towne Landing State Historic Site is that of the Ashley River.

The Ashley River served not only as an entry point but also as a settlement for English travelers.

- English travelers arrived during the late 1600s. This is when they established their formal settlements in Charleston.

- The establishment of the English community brought about the need to name the area where the travelers have settled in. It was first recognized as the Carolina colony from which many say the state's name originated.

20

Charleston Ghost Tours

Charleston has its share of ghost stories! There is no better way to enjoy a good Charleston ghost story than by going on a ghost tour.

Here are some of the best ghost tours in the city:

Ghostwalk

The first ghost tour company in Charleston, Ghostwalk has been operating since 1979. The tour includes exploring Charleston's French Quarter. You will hear local legends and ghost stories. The senior guide, Tricia (as of this publication), has been on A&E's *Flip this House* because of her expertise with the paranormal. Tricia is considered one of the most fascinating individuals in Charleston.

You can expect a lot of authentic low country charm and historical information. The tour is not scripted. Instead, you will hear stories from guides who have lived in Charleston and really know the area!

Black Cat Tours

This ghost tour involves exploring Charleston's dark, haunted, and odd history. You will be part of a small group of people on the tour. This way, each guest will get to more share of the fun and terror.

The tour is operated by Mark Jones and Rebel Sinclair (as of this publication), who are both investigators, authors, and historians. The tour caters to people who want to explore in relative privacy. It is ideal for the whole family.

Bulldog Ghost Tours

Bulldog Tours offers several different ghost tours. This tour company has exclusive access to some of Charleston's most haunted sites.

The Haunted Jail Tour will take you on a trip to the city's old jail. The Ghost & Dungeon Tour will have you follow a shadowy trail of churches, alleys, and cemeteries. The Darkside of Charleston Tour will introduce you to the city's history of prostitution, scandal, and crime.

21

Charleston Pirate Tours

If ghost stories aren't your thing, you might consider a pirate tour in Charleston. Pirate Tours are entertaining and provide a fun way to learn about Charleston.

Here are some of the pirate tours in Charleston:

Charleston Pirate Tours

This tour company features Charleston's most photographed tour guides and their pirates. All of the tours are walking tours around the city with a pirate tour guide! The tours include the Children's Treasure Hunt Tour, Pirate History Tour, Daytime Ghost Tour, and Pirate & Ghost Tour.

On the tours, you will learn about Blackbeard and why he blockaded the city's harbor. You will also learn how Charleston changed from a pirate ha-

ven to a favorite pirate target. You will also dis-
cover why Ann Bonny, a native of Charleston, fell
for Calico Jack Rackham and then became a pirate herself.

Pirates of Charleston

The Pirate Adventure Cruise will take you on a
thrilling high seas voyage deep into the heart of
the North Edisto River. Each kid gets to be a part
of the crew of the forty-five-foot pirate ship
called the Black Ghost. There is lots of singing
and nonstop action. Part of the adventure is
reading maps to find the hidden treasure.

The highlight of the tour is defeating Sneaky
Pete, who stole the key to the sunken treasure.
You will battle his crew with water cannons to get
the key back.

Captain Byrd's

In Pirates, Patriots, and Rebels, you will join his-
torian and author Captain Christopher Byrd
Downey in one of Charleston's premiere boat
tours. The trip will allow you to see the amazing
Charleston Harbor scenery, as you learn about
three hundred years of the city's amazing history.
Captain Byrd will astound you with stories about

some of the city's most famous, as well as most infamous, individuals who contributed to Charleston's rich maritime past.

You will experience what it felt like back when Blackbeard blockaded the harbor in 1718. The shots fired in 1881 that triggered the Civil War will echo in your ears. You will understand the significance of Charleston in one of US history's most defining moments.

Fun Facts about Charleston and Pirates

- Charleston is also one of the largest container ports in America, making it a feast for pirates in the early 1700s.

- There is a popular story in Charleston about the sea captain who would spear pineapples to his fence as a sign to his friends that he was safely home. This story explains how the pineapple became a symbol of hospitality.

22

Charleston Walking Tours

Another great way to see the city of Charleston is simply taking a walking tour. There are several companies that offer walking tours around Charleston:

Charleston Footprints

The tour this company offers is called the most comprehensive historic tour of Charleston. The tour guide, Michael Trouche, is a seventh-generation Charlestonian. He is an award-winning journalist and a two-time author. His two books about Charleston are *The Charm of Charleston: Architecture, Culture, and Nature* and *Charleston: Yesterday and Today*.

You will learn lots of fun historical facts on this tour, like amusing stories of Charleston's past, how the palmetto tree helped to shape the peninsula, and the history of the sweetgrass baskets.

Oyster Point Historic Walking Tours

Their two-hour tour is billed as the perfect introduction to the city for first-time visitors. The tour guides are local residents who have a love for the city.

Two Sisters Historic Walking Tours

This is a two-hour-and-fifteen-minute walking tour hosted by two sisters. Mary Ellen Dantzler and Therese Symthe are both seventh-generation Charlestonians. They grew up in Charleston, so they are able to share some stories and insight that others may not. The two sisters also share many funny stories about the history of Charleston.

Free Tours by Foot

This tour company offers a unique concept in a tour: no charge up front; you pay what the tour was worth to you in the end, even if you pay nothing.

The company offers three different walking tours: Historic Charleston, Civil War Charleston, and an Architecture Tour.

Thank You

Thank you for purchasing and taking the time to read this book.

This is the eighth in the Hey Kids! Let's Visit series of books for children.

If you and your children enjoyed the book or have any comments, I would love for you to review it on Amazon!

To keep in touch and be notified of the next books in the series, please join us at

http://kid-friendly-family-vacations.com/charlestonattractions

When you join us, you will receive a free gift!

If you enjoyed this book, I invite you to check out the other books in the Hey Kids! Let's Visit Series:

Hey Kids! Let's Visit Washington, DC
Hey Kids! Let's Visit a Cruise Ship
Hey Kids! Let's Visit New York City

Hey Kids! Let's Visit London, England
Hey Kids! Let's Visit San Francisco
Hey Kids! Let's Visit Savannah, Georgia
Hey Kids! Let's Visit Paris, France

Thanks Again!

Teresa Mills

Acknowledgements

Proof-reading / Editing
Deb Hall – TheWriteInsight.com

Cover Photos
Ravenel Bridge – © digidream / deposit photos

Patriots Point – Yorktown - © zhuzhu / deposit photos

Waterfront Park - © dndavis / deposit photos

Fort Sumter – cannons – personal vacation photo

Rainbow Row - © Wasin Pummarin / 123rf.com

Photos in Book
Fort Sumter - © Wollwerth / deposit photos

Fort Sumter – cannons – personal vacation photo

The Battery - © benkrut / deposit photos

Waterfront Park - © dndavis / deposit photos

City Market / Confederate Museum - © benkrut / deposit photos

Old Exchange & Provost Dungeon - © James Kirkikis / 123rf.com

Rainbow Row - © Wasin Pummarin / 123rf.com

Aquarium - sting ray - © rixipix / deposit photos

Dock Street Theater – © sepavone/ deposit photos

Patriots Point – Clamagore - © zhuzhu / deposit photos

Patriots Point – Yorktown - © zhuzhu / deposit photos

Ravenel Bridge (upclose) - © dcslim / deposit photos

Magnolia Plantation and Gardens – © daveallenphoto / 123rf.com

Middleton Place – © John C / 123rf.com

ABOUT THE AUTHOR

Teresa Mills is the best selling author of the "Hey Kids! Let's Visit..." Book Series for Kids!

Teresa's goal through her books and website is to help parents / grand-parents who want to build the life experiences of their children / grand-children through travel and learning activities.

She is an active mother and Mimi. She and her family love traveling in the USA, and internation-ally too! They love exploring new places, eating cool foods, and having yet another adventure as a family! With the Mills, it's all about traveling as family.

In addition to traveling, Teresa enjoys reading, hiking, biking, and helping others.

Join in the fun at http://kid-friendly-family-vacations.com

Made in the USA
Columbia, SC
05 January 2020